101 Amazing Facts about Natural Disasters

Jack Goldstein & Frankie Taylor

Published in 2015 by
AUK Authors, an imprint of
Andrews UK Limited
www.andrewsuk.com

Copyright © 2015 Jack Goldstein & Frankie Taylor

The rights of Jack Goldstein and Frankie Taylor to be identified as the authors of this work have been asserted in accordance with the Copyright, Designs and Patents Act 1988

All rights reserved. No part of this publication may be reproduced, stored in or introduced into a retrieval system, or transmitted, in any form, or by any means (electronic, mechanical, photocopying, recording or otherwise) without the prior written permission of the publisher. Any person who does any unauthorised act in relation to this publication may be liable to criminal prosecution and civil claims for damages.

All facts contained within this book have been researched from reputable sources. If any information is found to be false, please contact the publishers, who will be happy to make corrections for future editions.

Contents

Floods	1
Tropical Cyclones	6
Landslides & Avalanches	12
Tsunamis	19
Fires	25
Earthquakes	32
Blizzards	38
Heat Waves	43
Volcanoes	48
Lightning	52
And Finally...	58

Introduction

What exactly is an avalanche? Why do tropical cyclones spin in different directions? What is the deadliest heat wave ever to have been recorded? And what are the three different types of lightning? All of this and more is revealed in this fantastic book containing over one hundred facts about the world's most deadly natural disasters. Covering floods, cyclones, landslides, avalanches, tsunamis, fires, earthquakes, blizzards, heatwaves, volcanoes and lightning, this is a fascinating addition to any fact-lover's collection.

THE FACTS

Floods

- In the simplest possible terms, a flood is when water covers land that is *not* normally submerged. A flood can happen due to the overflow of water from a river or lake, or because there is too much rainwater for a given area of ground to drain away. Whereas some floods happen slowly, with the build-up taking place over an extended period of time, others happen very quickly; we refer to these as *flash floods*.

- The word *flood* that we use today comes from the Old English word *flot*, itself deriving from Latin words such as *fluctus* (translating as both *flood* and *disorder*) and *flumen* (a *river* or *stream*).

- Many cultures across the world feature stories of a flood sent by an angry deity, often with one sole 'good' man surviving the deluge. *The Epic of Gilgamesh* written in 700 BC tells of Utnapishtim, an immortal man who was instructed by the God Ea to build a huge boat in which he could save his family and the animals of the world from a huge flood which was about to destroy the world. Plato's *Timaeus* tells us that the God Zeus became angry at the Bronze race of humans who were constantly waging war, and decided to punish them with a flood. The Hebrew Bible speaks of Noah, the one righteous man saved from the flood along with his family and the animals of the earth when he builds an ark.

- There are five key categories of flood. An *areal* flood is caused by rainfall, where ground is saturated and the falling water cannot run off quickly enough. A *riverine* flood is one where a river breaks its banks due to an increased amount of water finding its way into the river upstream. A combination of winds and low pressure can cause a sea tidal surge – an *estuarine* flood, and *urban flooding* is that caused by rainfall overwhelming the capacity of human-made drainage systems. The last type is the *catastrophic* flood, which is caused by a major event such as an earthquake, volcanic eruption or even the bursting of a dam.

▶ Floods can be both negative and positive events. Many countries carefully manage their flood defences, as it can be hugely costly to repair the damage when a river bursts its banks near to a built-up area, and it is devastating to farms that are within the flood plain. However, some communities – especially the ancient civilizations along rivers such as the Nile, Ganges and Indus rivers – relied on periodic flooding for their livelihoods. A flood will make soil more fertile, increasing its nutrients, and can even kill pests in arid farmland.

▶ The 1931 China floods are considered to be among the deadliest natural disasters ever to have affected the human race. The two previous years had seen extreme droughts, until the winter of 1930 and the heavy snowstorms that it brought. Rains in the spring saw river levels rise significantly, and these continued – along with cyclone activity – through the summer. In July and August of 1931 there were nine cyclones that affected the region, and both the Yangtze and Huai Rivers overflowed with catastrophic effects, especially when the waters reached Nanjing, China's capital at the time. Around four million people died either of drowning or of the severe cholera and typhus epidemics that followed.

- Both in 1887 and 1938, China's Yellow River flooded with great loss of life. The river runs within elevated dykes surrounded with broad plains, and on both of these occasions the river's flow increased so heavily that it burst its banks swamping agricultural and commercial areas. In 1887 an estimated one million people drowned, with a further million killed by starvation and disease; exactly the same problems resulted in a death toll of 700,000 just over fifty years later.

- In 1975, a flood classified as 'once in 2000 years' occurred as a result of Typhoon Nina. The Banqiao Dam had been engineered to withstand extreme water levels – but no-one had foreseen the terrible conditions that this particular typhoon would bring. The weather had caused communication lines to the dam to fail, and when the message to open the dam was sent, it was not heeded. As more and more water piled in from upstream, the sluice gates could not handle the overflow, and the wave protection wall failed. Seven hundred million cubic metres of water rushed over the dam in just six hours, resulting in a wave more than six miles wide and seven metres high, travelling at more than thirty miles per hour. More than 85,000 people died in the flood, and almost 150,000 lost their lives to disease soon afterwards.

- A flood that occurred on St Felix's day – Saturday the 6th of November – in 1530 caused that particular day to be renamed *Evil Saturday* in the Netherlands. The country is famous for its low-lying land, and many lessons were learned about the power of the weather when large parts of Flanders and Zeeland

were completely washed away, resulting in the loss of some 100,000 lives. Today, flood defence technology there is some of the most advanced in the world; the country's people never want to see a repeat of Evil Saturday again.

► Throughout this section we have spoken about floods of water. But this final fact is about a rather unusual – but still devastating flood. On January the 15th 1919, a storage tank burst, and its contents of molasses (also called black treacle) rushed through the streets of Boston, Massachusetts at thirty-five miles per hour. Twenty-one people died in the flood, and around one hundred and fifty people were injured. Legend has it that on a hot summer day, you can still smell the sickly sweet aroma of treacle in the city!

TROPICAL CYCLONES

- A tropical cyclone is a storm system with certain characteristics – it rotates rapidly, consists of strong winds, has an area of low pressure at the centre (which we call the *eye*) and features a spiral arrangement of thunderstorms which produce an extremely high amount of rain. Across the world, tropical cyclones are known by different names, including *tropical depression, hurricane, cyclonic storm* and *typhoon*. Whatever name is used, a tropical cyclone usually reaches anywhere between 60 and 2500 miles in diameter.

- A tropical cyclone usually forms over a large body of warm water. The water evaporates from the ocean's surface, cooling as it rises and recondenses into rain clouds. Due to the vertical direction of the airflow and a property of physics called *the conservation of angular momentum*, the earth's rotation (in an example of the *Coriolis effect)* causes the winds to form in a circular motion. Because of this, they rarely form over the equator (where there is no rotational effect) and generally only form in tropical seas – in fact, this is why they are called *tropical* cyclones! Due to this effect, the winds of a cyclone blow *anticlockwise* in the northern hemisphere and *clockwise* in the southern hemisphere.

- Tropical cyclones are not only dangerous because of their high wind speed, but also because of what this speed can cause – high waves, storm surges (coastal floods with similar characteristics to a tsunami) and tornadoes (rapidly rotating columns of air that can actually lift entire buildings into the sky). They are most dangerous in coastal regions, as the further they move inland, the further away from their energy source they become – and therefore weaken in strength.

- The eye of a cyclone is formed because the wind at the centre sinks to the ground, suppressing the formation of any clouds. Although the *weather* inside the eye is usually calm, the *sea* is not necessarily so – in fact contrary to popular belief it can often be extremely violent! Although normally between 20 and 40 miles in diameter, the largest eyes can reach over 200 miles wide. The outer edge of the eye is known as the *eyewall* and it is here that the fastest winds within the cyclone are found. The most devastating cyclones (to humans) are those where the eyewall passes over land we use.

- Ways in which we measure tropical cyclones include *intensity*, which is defined as the maximum wind speed in the storm over a one-minute or ten-minute average, and various measurements of size, such as the radius of maximum wind, the radius of wind at gale-force levels and the radius of the outermost closed isobar (line of equal or constant pressure). Different agencies have different naming conventions for tropical cyclones; for instance the American National Hurricane Centre classes a cyclone with one-minute sustained winds of 95 knots as a 'category 2 hurricane', whereas the Australian Bureau of Meteorology say that a category 2 tropical cyclone is anything that reaches just 71 knots sustained for one minute. Everyone pretty much agrees however that the *highest* class of tropical cyclone occurs when one-minute sustained winds reach over 130 knots!

Cyclone Catarina as seen from the International Space Station in 2004

▶ The deadliest tropical cyclone ever recorded is the *Bhola* cyclone that struck what is now Bangladesh and West Bengal in India on the 12th of November 1970. The cyclone caused a storm surge which flooded the majority of the low-lying islands in the Ganges delta, killing an estimated half a million people. The cyclone had formed over the Bay of Bengal four days earlier, and travelled north, reaching a peak wind speed of 115 miles per hour on the 11th of November. Crops were destroyed and whole villages were washed away; in Tazumuddin nearly half of the population – some 85,000 people – lost their lives.

- The most devastating recent tropical cyclone was *Cyclone Nargis,* which in 2008 caused the worst natural disaster ever to affect the country of Myanmar. As with the Bhola cyclone it was the storm surge that did the most damage, this time sending flood waters some thirty miles up the Irrawaddy delta causing around 140,000 people to lose their lives almost instantly. Thankfully, relief efforts saw that – in a contrast with many similar natural disasters of years gone by – there was *not* a second wave of tens of thousands of deaths due to disease and starvation. Although the *human* cost could never be expressed in monetary terms, the damage to the country's infrastructure was estimated to be the equivalent of ten billion US dollars.

- Whereas most of the deadliest fifty cyclones of all time occurred in the Bay of Bengal or West Pacific, one – known as the *Great Hurricane* took 22,000 lives in the Atlantic in 1780. Many islands in the Caribbean suffered terrible losses of life when the storm passed through the area. When it struck Barbados, winds in excess of 200 miles per hour were experienced before the storm made its way past Martinique, Saint Lucia and many other islands of the Antilles. The year was a particularly bad one in the region, with two more deadly storms hitting the area badly later in the same month – particularly bad news for the British fleet, who not only were in the middle of fighting the American Revolution but were also wrestling for control of the area with the French.

- The most *intense* tropical cyclone officially measured to date – based on the maximum speed of one-minute sustained surface winds – was *Typhoon Haiyan* (known in the Philippines, the area in which it struck as *Typhoon Yolanda*). Winds of 90 m/s (195 mph) were recorded, although gusts reached above 200 miles per hour. Incredibly however, the gusts of *Cyclone Olivia* in 1996 reached an astonishing 253 miles per hour!

- The longest lasting tropical cyclone was *Typhoon John*, which lasted for 31 days between the 11th of August and the 10th of September 1994. The largest cyclone recorded was *Typhoon Tip* in October 1979, whose winds extended out 1380 miles from the centre. However the costliest tropical cyclone ever is the terrible *Hurricane Katrina* which formed in the western Atlantic and devastated the Gulf of Mexico, causing $108 billion dollars of damage at the time.

Landslides & Avalanches

- A landslide is a large volume of rock and other ground elements fall down a slope under the effect of gravity – although, importantly, there are certain conditions which lead a certain area to be prone to 'failure', with a trigger event setting off the actual event, which is also often called a land*slip*. Factors which contribute to the potential for a landslide include excessive groundwater pressure, loss of vegetation (such as after a fire), erosion by rivers or oceans, saturation from snow, rain or glaciers, recent earthquakes and volcanic eruptions.

- Although the conditions that lead to a landslide are more often than not caused by nature, there are certain actions taken *by humans* which increase the danger of an unplanned landslide. Deforestation will have a similar effect to that of loss of vegetation after a wildfire, and blasting or earthworks can reflect natural earthquakes. More unseen threats are posed by vibration from traffic or machinery which can loosen soil in readiness for a landslide, or construction activities that alter the amount of water entering the soil.

- There are a number of main landslide classifications. A *debris flow* (also known as a *mud flow*) occurs when a slope has been saturated by water; the debris can temporarily block the flow of water – however when the blockages fail, a domino effect is created and the flow can increase dramatically in intensity. *Earthflows* are similar in nature to *debris flows*, however rather than water they occur when the slope material is fine-grained, such as clay, fine sand or silt. A debris *slide* is different to a debris *flow* in that it usually starts with the movement of large rocks at the top of the slope, which break down as they fall; this will be much slower than the water-saturated *flow*. When the sliding surface is located within the soil mantle – usually no more than a few metres deep – we call this a *shallow landslide,* whereas if the sliding surface is below the deepest tree roots (often more than ten metres below the surface) it is referred to as a *deep-seated landslide*. One final classification is the *Sturzstorm*, a little-understood type of landslide which is very mobile, flowing over low angles of terrain – and sometimes even uphill.

- Landslides are related to another type of natural disaster featured in this book – Tsunamis. One of the key causes of a tsunami is a landslide that occurs under the surface of the water. At the extreme end of the scale, the largest landslides have in fact been known to cause what geologists call *megatsunamis*. There is also a phenomenon known as a *pyroclastic flow*, which is essentially a fusion of ash, rocks and gas that is ejected from an active volcano and forms a type of landslide down its side. Of all landslides these are perhaps the most terrifying, as the addition of fiery hot matter to an already frightening occurrence is surely one of the planet's worst horrors.

- An *avalanche* is a type of landslide that mainly contains snow. They are usually triggered by a loss of cohesion in one of the layers of snow that has accumulated on a mountain, when the forces applied (usually purely by gravity) are in excess of the holding strength of the layer. As the avalanche picks up more snow, this increases its weight and force, thus causing even more snow layers to lose their grip, come loose and join the avalanche. The result is a rapidly increasing fall of snow that can pick up trees and rocks as it makes its way down the mountain. It is a myth that shouting loudly can cause an avalanche (in fact, sound waves are far too weak to have any effect), and avalanches are *not* in fact rare events – almost every mountain with standing snow is likely to suffer them on an ongoing basis.

► The people of Wales will never forget the Aberfan disaster. On the 21st of October 1966, a build-up of water in the spoil tip of a local colliery caused it to collapse, turning the rock and shale into a fast-moving slurry. Within just minutes, 40,000 cubic metres of this debris had covered the village of Aberfan which stood at the bottom of the mountain, and 116 children along with 28 adults had been killed. The horror and sadness of that day has never left the village which lost more than half its children in just a few terrible minutes.

► In 1963, on the 9th of October, 260 million cubic metres of rock were loosened from Mount Toc in Northern Italy, crashing into the reservoir below. The locals were well aware of the mountain's tendency to suffer from landslips, referring to it as *The Walking Mountain*. No-one foresaw the scale of *this* particular event however. Such was the volume of debris that fell into the reservoir that a wave 250 metres high smashed over the dam wall, hurtling into the valley below. Almost two thousand men, women and children lost their lives as the town of Longarone and its suburbs were almost entirely swept away by the water.

An avalanche taking place on Mount Everest

- On the 23rd of February 1999, an avalanche began on an Alpine slope in Austria. Within just sixty seconds it had reached more than fifty metres in height and was travelling at nearly two hundred miles per hour. The village of Galtür had been separated into zones based on risk from such events – yet it was the safest 'green' zones into which this massively powerful powder avalanche smashed, overturning cars, collapsing buildings, and burying 57 people. Despite heroic efforts by rescue crews and locals, thirty-one people had lost their lives. Analysis of the cause of this particular tragedy led scientists to discover a previously-unknown layer of impacted snow called the *saltation layer*; it is hoped that understanding the circumstances which led to the Galtür Avalanche will help prevent similar tragedies occurring elsewhere.

- The most devastating landslide from a human perspective was surely the *Vargas Tragedy*. Vargas is a state in Venezuela, which, on the 15th of December 1999 was beset by torrential rain. Although the area was used to mud slides of a certain size, the storm this time was exceptional – nearly a *whole metre* of rain fell in just a few days, causing soil instability on a massive scale. Huge debris flows combined with flash floods, and millions of tons of rocks, soil, trees and dirt came crashing down the mountains from every angle. With three-metre thick flows reaching astonishing speeds of up to 15 metres per second, many areas stood no chance. Some towns just completely disappeared – Cerro Grande and Carmen de Uria suffered this awful fate; other neighbourhoods remained in place but were buried under metres of mud. Although exact figures have never been established, it is thought that up to ten per cent of the region's population – around thirty thousand people – lost their lives in the truly horrific event.

- Despite our knowledge of landslides, and the use of all kinds of technologies from satellite imaging to advanced computer modelling, people in certain areas today are *still* at risk from landslides. In March 2014, a portion of an unstable hill roughly four miles east of Oso in America's Washington State collapsed, engulfing a small neighbourhood in mud and debris. An area roughly one square mile in size was covered, and forty-three people lost their lives. There was local controversy when the director of the local Department of Emergency management said the tragic event was 'completely unforeseen', yet

The *Seattle Times had* published an article that very same day which highlighted the area as a hot-spot for landslides, referencing a recent study that warned how the hillside that eventually collapsed was one of the most dangerous in the country.

Tsunamis

Still from a 2009 video showing a tsunami hitting a parking lot in American Samoa

- A *tsunami* is a series of waves caused by water disturbances such as earthquakes, volcanic eruptions, calving (when large chunks of ice break off a glacier's edge), landslides or underwater explosions.

- Tsunamis generally occur in oceans and large lakes and differ from normal sea waves due to their wavelengths being much longer. Unlike everyday 'wind waves' which can reach heights of around 2 metres, tsunamis can top 25 metres in height. The highest tsunami wave ever recorded occurred in Alaska's Lituya Bay in 1958 and was measured as being an astonishing 30 metres tall.

- The word tsunami means harbour wave in Japanese, and has essentially been adopted worldwide as the common word used to describe this natural phenomenon. Until recently, English-speaking countries referred to these events as tidal waves, and scientists may still describe them as seismic sea waves.

- Although even today our understanding of tsunamis is limited, a Greek historian named Thucydides wrote that the phenomenon was caused by underwater earthquakes around 2500 years ago. It was however only in the late 20th century that scientists began to properly appreciate the mechanics of these often devastating events.

- Scientists today are still trying to find out why some large earthquakes do not cause even the smallest tsunami, yet small earthquakes can sometimes result in absolutely devastating ones. Even with our increasing understanding of how they travel across the oceans, it is perhaps the fact that much about tsunamis remains unknown that makes them one of today's most feared natural disasters.

- The most deadly tsunami in modern times took place on the 26th of December 2004, and was caused by an earthquake reaching a magnitude over nine on the *Moment Magnitude* scale (making the earthquake itself the third most powerful ever recorded). In the open ocean the resulting tidal wave measured just one metre in height, yet as it reached the shores this increased to a terrifying fifteen metres. The Sumatran region which took the brunt of the tsunami was not experienced or in any way prepared for the events of that day. With almost no warning the wave hit the region, wiping away homes and public buildings, devastating the Indonesian region before travelling onto Thailand and further afield. In total it seriously affected fourteen countries, claimed the lives of around two hundred thousand people and made some two million more homeless. As a direct result of the event, the countries surrounding the Indian Ocean have set up an early warning system which hopes to minimise the impact of future similar events.

- When Krakatoa erupted on the 27th of August 1883, the resulting tsunami saw waves some thirty-seven metres high hit nearby shores, killing an estimated forty thousand people even though the surrounding areas were much less densely populated then. The eruption and tsunami were so powerful that even Sri Lanka suffered fatalities, and the shore at Bombay receded.

- On the 11th of March 2011, an earthquake of magnitude nine occurred off the coast of Eastern Japan. Less than an hour later, a devastating tsunami followed. Although scientists were in fact expecting an earthquake at the time, no-one had predicted the sheer scale of what nature produced that day, and no-one had thought there was a realistic chance of a dangerous tsunami occurring as a result of it. Yet happen it did. The waves reached run-up heights of thirty-nine metres, overtopping and destroying seawalls put in place to protect Japan from such an event. Buildings as tall as three storeys high (many where people had taken refuge) were destroyed, and humans weren't the only species affected – more than ten thousand nesting seabirds were wiped out by a wave that had crossed the Pacific Ocean to the Midway Atoll National Wildlife Refuge, one of the oldest atoll formations in the world. Back in Japan, five million tons of debris was washed back out to sea, much of which continues to turn up on American and Canadian shores to this day. Perhaps the most worrying event that day was the state of emergency declared at the Fukushima nuclear power plant. When the earthquake struck, generators were pumping water which cooled the nuclear reactor units; the resulting tsunami knocked out the generators causing the reactors to overheat. With 300 tons of radioactive water leaking out on a daily basis, the accident has since been classified as equal in severity to the 1986 Chernobyl disaster. The overall cost of the tsunami to Japan's economy is believed to have run into many tens of billions of US dollars.

Six weeks after the 2004 tsunami hit the island of Sumatra, Indonesia, it was still difficult to tell where the sea stopped and the land begun.

- The tsunami that followed the *Great Lisbon Earthquake* terrified the occupants of Portugal's capital in 1755. When the five-minute long earthquake struck, many people made their way to the harbour area where they believed they would be safe. However, forty minutes later they watched the water recede (allowing them to glimpse a never-before-seen seabed littered with shipwrecks and lost cargo) before a tidal wave came crashing towards them. That was followed by *two* further tsunamis in quick succession, all of which raced up the Tagus river causing further devastation. Where water did not strike, fires broke out, with flames raging for five whole days. It is thought that up to forty thousand inhabitants of Lisbon lost their lives that day (the 1st of November – All Saints' Day), with another 10,000 in Morocco (which was also struck as a result of the earthquake and following tsunamis) succumbing to the same fate. In addition to the human cost, there were great cultural losses, with hundreds of priceless works of art housed in the city's royal library being destroyed.

- The tsunami that occurred after the *1960 Valdivia Earthquake* (the most powerful earthquake ever recorded) affected not only Chile but also Hawaii, Japan, the Philippines, Eastern New Zealand, Southeast Australia, and the Aleutian Islands. The coast of Chile between 38 and 45 degrees latitude was utterly devastated, damaging port infrastructure and causing huge loss of life. The tsunami raced across the Pacific Ocean at a speed of hundreds of kilometres per hour, killing seven people in Hilo on the island of Hawaii. Even today you can still see the wrecks of vessels which were damaged during the events of that day.

Fires

A wildfire in the Bitterroot National Forest in Montana, United States

- A fire is a process whereby a material is rapidly oxidated through combustion, releasing heat and light as well as certain other products of the reaction. The part of the process you can actually *see* is the flame, which – depending on the substance that is alight – will burn with various colours and intensities. The ability to make and control fire is considered to be one of the biggest changes in early human history, and the latest evidence suggests that fire could have been used in a controlled way up to a million years ago – although it is around 100,000 years ago that the practice appears to have become more commonplace.

- In a natural disaster context, fires that are beyond our control can prove utterly devastating. Whether they begin without our intervention (as wildfires generally do), or are initiated by us (for instance in the WWII bombing of Dresden), fires can become some of the most terrifying and deadly events.

- A fire requires starting; this happens when a combustible material in the presence of oxygen (or an oxygen-rich compound) is heated above its *flash point* – the lowest temperature at which the mixture of the material and the oxidizer will vaporize to form an ignitable mixture in the air.

- The fire also requires a *chain reaction* to continue; this is achieved when the fire sustains its oxidation by supplying enough heat to continue *without any added external heat.* This ongoing stage of a fire requires continuous heat, fuel and oxygen; take away any of those elements and the fire will cease burning. The role of gravity in a fire should not be underestimated; in most fires where the source of oxygen is the surrounding air, gravity is responsible for convection, removing the products of combustion and bringing a fresh supply of oxygen. It is interesting to note therefore that without gravity, a fire will quickly surround itself with the products of combustion, ensuring oxygen cannot reach it – and therefore extinguishing itself. This means that the risk of fire in a spacecraft is actually very low!

► Whether through controlled burns (such as the burning of a certain agricultural area to clear overgrown areas and release valuable nutrients back into the soil, or perhaps creating a natural barrier to prevent wildfires from spreading further than a particular area) or by totally natural blazes, an area of almost two million square miles is burned across the world in any given year – an incredible amount considering that the entire USA is only twice that size!

► Australia's worst ever bushfire disasters – now referred to as the *Black Saturday Bushfires* – occurred on Saturday the 7th of February 2009 in the state of Victoria. For a whole week, southeastern Australia had been suffering an exceptional heatwave; Melbourne for instance saw three days where the temperature peaked above 43 degrees centigrade, and one day (the third hottest in its history) at just over 45 degrees. The whole state was tinder-dry, and as Saturday approached, all signs pointed towards a day of the most extreme weather that would be perfect for starting wildfires. Come Saturday itself, thousands of firefighters were dispatched to deal with the expected fires – yet no-one could have battled nature effectively on a day which saw temperatures in Melbourne hit 46.4 degrees (still a record to this day), humidity levels drop to an incredible six per cent, and winds reach sixty miles per hour. Some four hundred individual fires were recorded during the day, which resulted in Australia's highest ever loss of life from bushfires: despite heroic efforts from everyone concerned, 173 people died that day.

► One of the most controversial acts of World War II was the bombing of the German city of Dresden by America and Britain between the 13th and the 15th of February 1945. The USAF said the attack was a justified bombing of a major military and industrial target; others declared it an act of cultural vandalism and genocide. The bombing was of such intensity that hundreds – if not thousands – of small fires started, before joining up into one huge conflagration. This huge city-wide fire attained such an intensity that it sustained its own wind system, fuelling itself with more and more oxygen as the gale force winds blew towards the centre from every point on the compass. The fire burned everything that it possibly could, turning the very surface of the streets into a flammable liquid. The terrifying scene is one of the most hellish ever created by man (not dissimilar to that immediately after the atomic bomb was dropped on Hiroshima) and resulted in a shocking number of deaths; the exact figure is not known but is estimated to have been between twenty-five and one hundred thousand innocent German civilians.

Australian Bushfires in 2003

▶ Many Americans know of the *Great Chicago Fire* which destroyed over three square miles of Chicago and killed some 300 people on the days around the 8th October 1871. Yet it was in fact *another* fire that occurred that day which could be called the *worst* in American history. It was described by Novelist Denise Gess and historian William Lutz as "nature's nuclear explosion – a wall of flame a mile high, five miles wide, travelling at 100 miles per hour, hotter than a crematorium turning sand to glass." That description of *The Peshtigo Fire* (which occurred in and around Peshtigo, Wisconsin) is so powerful that little else can be said – only that the 2,500 deaths it caused means that even today it remains the greatest loss of life by fire in one event in the entirety of American history.

- Perhaps the most famous of all city fires, the *Great Fire of London* took place between Sunday the 2nd and Wednesday the 5th of September 1666. Starting at Thomas Farriner's bakery on Pudding Lane, the fire gutted almost the entire medieval city of London (situated inside the old Roman city wall), consuming over thirteen thousand houses, eighty-seven churches and Old St Paul's Cathedral. The fire did not *quite* reach either the rich districts of Westminster or Whitehall, nor the poor suburban slums, but still left some 80,000 inhabitants homeless. It has traditionally been said that just six people died in the fire, however although it is true that only six deaths were *officially* recorded, a great number of poor and even middle-class people are likely to have been killed without mention, and the heat of the fire would have essentially cremated many without even leaving any discernible remains. Despite proposals to rebuild the city on a grid system – a suggestion which would have helped traffic flow even to this very day – residents quickly rebuilt the streets essentially to the exact same medieval plan as before the fire… after all, they were more keen to get a roof over their head than worry about how long a taxi across the city would take some four hundred years later!

- One rather unusual fire is that which burns under the ghost-town of Centralia in Pennsylvania, USA. In 1962, five members of the volunteer fire company were hired to clean up the town landfill. As had been the case in previous years, the men set the dump on fire and let it burn. Unlike previous years however, the fire was not put out… and found its way through an unsealed opening nearby into the miles of abandoned coal mines beneath the city (although it should be noted that there are other theories as to how it actually started). The fire was known to be burning down there, but it was mostly forgotten about. Until... fifteen years later, the owner of a gas station (and town mayor) put a dipstick in his underground tanks to check their level. When he pulled it out, the stick was warm, so he lowered down a thermometer on a string. When *that* came back up, he was astonished to see the temperature of the gasoline was some 77.8 degrees centigrade! Incredibly – and despite incidents such as a young boy falling into a fiery sinkhole and only narrowly being rescued – it took another *thirteen* years to convince most of the residents to leave. We say 'most' because even though the area was – and is still – home to deadly pockets of carbon monoxide, some stayed even after this... in 2009 a number of residents were *still* refusing to leave! And, of course, the fire is still burning...

Earthquakes

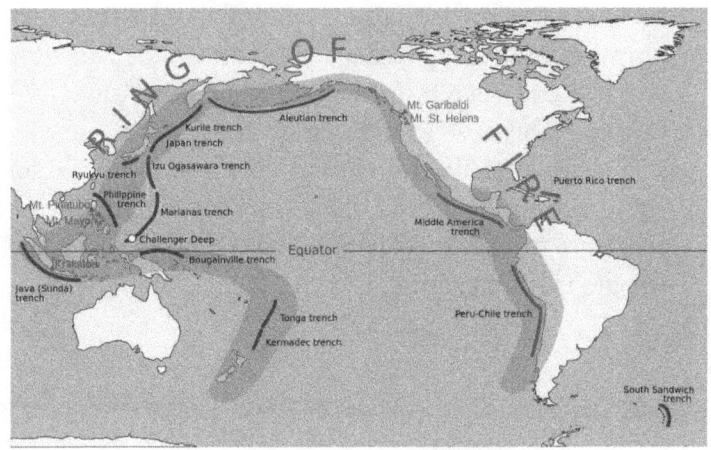

The Pacific Ring of Fire

- An earthquake is a shaking of the surface of the earth that is strong enough to be perceptible to humans. Also known as *quakes*, *tremors* or *temblors*, some have been so violent that they have destroyed whole cities, whereas others are barely even felt. The exact point at which an earthquake's rupture occurs is called the *hypocentre*. The more commonly-used term epicentre is actually the point at ground level which is directly above the *hypocentre*.

- The strength of an earthquake is today described by the *Moment Magnitude Scale*, which measures the size of the event in terms of energy released. This replaced the well-known *Richter Scale* in the 1970s and many media reports today *still* confuse the two (often announcing a quake is a particular number 'on the Richter scale'). The *new* scale was in fact designed to class magnitudes similarly to the older and more widely recognised one, so any difference as a result of using the wrong scale is actually quite minor.

- Earthquakes are generally the result of natural causes, the most common being the rupture of geological faults, however the word does still apply to seismic events that are the result of alternative causes, such as volcanic activity, landslides and even nuclear blasts. The 'standard' type of earthquake is called a tectonic earthquake and is caused by the release of stored strain energy where the sides of a fault plane 'break through' after having been stuck against each other whilst their respective plates continue to move.

- There are three main fault types: *normal*, *thrust* (also called reverse) and *strike-slip*. Normal and thrust faults occur when the displacement along the fault is in the direction of the dip – this results in the movement having a *vertical* element to it. On the other hand, strike-slip faults occur when the two sides of the fault slip *horizontally* past each other. Of course, many earthquakes are not exclusively just one type of these, and therefore have components of both normal/thrust and strike-slip – we call these *oblique slip faults*.

- Scientists believe that around half a million detectable earthquakes occur each year, around a fifth of which are felt by occupants of the areas in which they occur. Many places such as California, Mexico, Pakistan and others experience almost constant earthquakes, although most are at a very low level. There are thousands of seismic stations positioned around the world which detect earthquakes, most of which (in fact almost 90%) occur in a horseshoe-shaped zone forty thousand kilometres long known as the *Pacific Ring of Fire*.

- The *Great Lisbon Earthquake* stuck Portugal during the morning of the 1st of November 1755, a day celebrated among the Roman Catholic Church (and a number of protestant denominations) as *All Saints Day*. At the time the earthquake struck, many were attending mass; sadly the historic churches in which they were worshipping were unable to withstand the force and collapsed, leaving those inside either dead or injured. The quake (which had an estimated magnitude of around 8.9) left Lisbon in ruins, with

The aftermath of the 1906 San Francisco earthquake

fissures some fifteen feet wide tearing open the city's centre. Theologians focused on the religious cause and message, seeing it as a clear act of God. The city's philosophers however rubbished this idea, pointing out that the city's red light district suffered only minor damage!

▶ An earthquake in Kamchatka, Russia on the 4th of November 1952 measured 9.0 on the Moment Magnitude Scale, and caused a tsunami that saw nine-metre high waves crash into Hawaii. Thankfully there was no reported loss of human life despite the quake being one of the strongest ever recorded – although a farmer on Oahu did report the unfortunate loss of six cows that were swept back out to sea. Other notable quakes where lives were sadly lost include the 1923 Great Earthquake in Japan (150,000 deaths), the 1906 San Francisco quake (3000 deaths). Perhaps the most unusual series of quakes ever is the 1811-1812 Missouri Earthquakes which actually caused the Mississippi river to flow backwards!

- The 1960 *Valdivia Earthquake* is currently the most powerful earthquake to have ever been recorded on the *Moment Magnitude Scale*, reaching a quite shocking 9.5. On the afternoon of Sunday the 22nd of May, the earthquake struck, lasting around ten minutes. Considering that a 'normal' earthquake often lasts just seconds, one can imagine just how devastating this one would prove to be. The quake was so massive that even its foreshocks (which took place the previous day) were of a 7.9 magnitude – in fact many thought the foreshocks were the 'main' quake. The epicentre was near a town named Lumaco, with Valdivia being the most affected city; half of its buildings were uninhabitable as a direct result of the disaster. The death toll of the quake is almost impossible to determine, as a tsunami stuck just 15 minutes later, killing some forty thousand people.

- On the 28th of March 1964, an earthquake of magnitude 9.2 occurred in Prince William Sound in Alaska – the second most powerful in recorded history. Thankfully, due to its remoteness, only 128 lives were lost (although of course *any* loss of life is a human tragedy). The quake was felt all over Alaska and even further afield in Canada, with the city of Anchorage (eighty miles away from the epicentre) suffering around three hundred million dollars worth of damage.

- On the 25th of April 2015, Nepal experienced its worst earthquake in over eighty years. Historical monuments and buildings were destroyed and entire villages were wiped out with thousands left homeless. With a magnitude of more than 8.0 and a hypocentre only fifteen kilometres below the surface (the shallower the depth, the more devastating an equivalent quake is), it is believed that around eight thousand people lost their lives and more than twenty-three thousand were injured. The earthquake was so violent it caused an avalanche on nearby Mount Everest which killed nineteen people – making it the deadliest day on the mountain in recorded history. In addition to this, more than two hundred people were reported missing after a second avalanche was triggered in a region of the Himalayas known as Langtang. Aftershocks continued throughout Nepal in ten to fifteen minute intervals, with an additional large quake occurring seventeen days later – again taking the lives of many innocent people. Seismologist Vinod Kumar Gaur had predicted that the region would suffer from a major quake just a few years prior, yet it was claimed that some government officials believed that because a large earthquake had struck in 1934, there was no chance of *another* one happening so soon (in seismological terms) afterwards.

Blizzards

Utility poles in North Dakota almost completely buried by snow.

- The 'official' definition of a blizzard is a snowstorm with sustained winds above thirty-five miles per hour that lasts for more than three hours from start to finish. Although this is generally accepted to be snow that is *falling* from the sky, there is also a condition known as a *ground blizzard* in which a similar effect is created by the winds whipping up already-settled snow.

- In addition to the extreme cold and the possibility of getting snowed in – be that in a car, house or elsewhere – one of the largest dangers posed by blizzards is that they can severely reduce visibility. This makes driving in such conditions extremely treacherous and ill-advised.

- Blizzards can be one of the most disorientating weather conditions an individual can experience. Because of the similarity between the colour of the ground and the sky, the horizon can actually disappear (at least to *our* eyes) as normal reference points are covered up. This particular effect of a blizzard is known as a *white-out*.

- As mentioned above, blizzards bring with them extremely low temperatures. The *actual* temperature – usually below minus ten degrees centigrade – feels a great deal colder due to the *wind chill factor*, often making conditions seem closer to minus thirty or less! There is a real risk of death due to hypothermia in these extremes and some regions (especially if they are not used to such events) can suffer terribly as communication lines will have also gone down. The key advice for dealing with a blizzard is almost ridiculously simple – *be prepared*.

1888 saw America face more blizzards - thankfully though, not quite as bad as eight years before!

- One word you may hear that is related to blizzards (especially in Canada and northern parts of the USA) is *snowsquall*. This is best described as a more localised blizzard – a snowfall which begins suddenly and is characterised by strong, gusting surface winds. Whereas a blizzard will *always* result in settling snow, a snowsquall may be purely based in the air itself.

- The deadliest blizzard in recorded history is the 1972 *Iran Blizzard*. Two hundred Iranian villages were covered in up to eight metres of snow after falls lasting an entire week without respite. An area bigger than the whole of England was completely and utterly covered in snow, and four thousand people lost their lives from hypothermia, starvation and suffocation.

- No American alive today could remember the *Snow Winter* of 1880. But older men and women may have heard stories passed down by *their* grandparents who witnessed it first-hand. The snow first arrived in October 1880, and when blizzard after blizzard followed, the country – only recently having been opened up by the railroads – effectively came to a halt. Whole families struggled to survive, many rarely venturing out of their homes, most of which were buried up to their roofs in the snow. One railroad company hired men to dig out the tracks, yet by the time they had freed one section, the previous one would be covered again. No winter thaw came, and a few months later a *second* set of blizzards tormented the country for nine whole days; farmers now had to tunnel through the snow to reach the barns in which their livestock – and their livelihood – were housed. When the snow finally melted in May 1881, whole towns were washed away by the torrents of water that were created.

- In more recent times, the *Great blizzard of 1993* is still spoken of in some areas of America; it is often called the *Storm of the Century*. This cyclone stretched from Canada to central America, depositing two feet of snow in areas such as Alabama and Georgia, with even the traditionally warmest areas of Florida getting their share (which was an incredible four inches!) The hurricane-force winds and storm surges killed many people, and saw some ten million Americans go without power for extended periods of time.

- The winter of 1946/47 brought the worst snow since the Victorian era in Britain. The Second World War (which had only ended the previous year) had left coal supplies very low in the country, and some power stations had to shut down because not enough fuel could be brought to them. Domestic electricity supply was cut to just nineteen hours a day, and was altogether halted to certain industries. Radio broadcasts were limited, television was stopped completely, newspapers were published in smaller sizes and some magazines were not produced at all. The severity of this particular winter saw the pound actually devalue from four dollars to under three, and is considered by some historians as signifying (and to some extent causing, or at least finalising) Britain's decline as a world superpower.

- China's worst recent blizzards came in 2008, when a series of winter storms affected huge swathes of central and southern areas of the country. 129 deaths were directly attributed to the weather conditions, which saw over two hundred thousand homes destroyed, nearly a million damaged, power outages in cities such as Chenzhou (with a population of nearly five million) that lasted a whole two weeks, and hundreds of thousands of people without running water.

Heat Waves

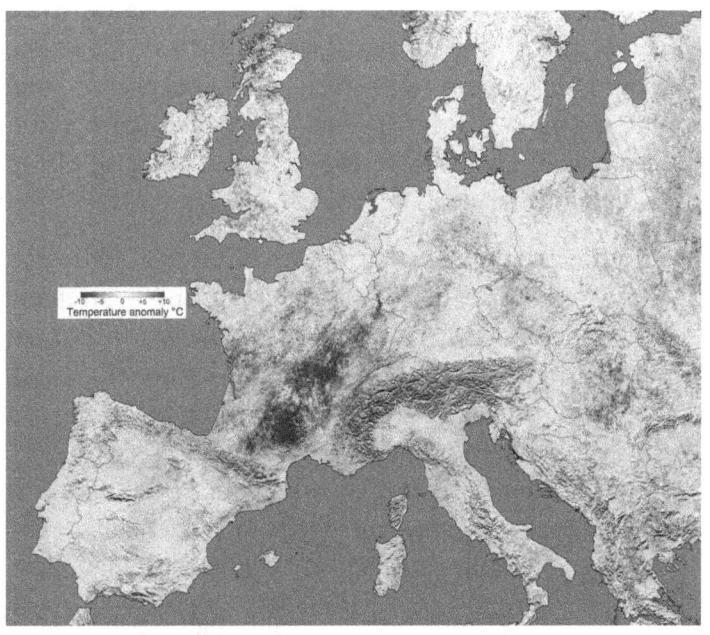

Europe experienced a heatwave in 2003. This map shows the differences in day time land surface temperatures between that year and 2001.

- There is in fact no 'official' definition of what constitutes a heatwave. The critical factor is that it is an extended period of sustained hot weather that is greater in temperature than what can normally be expected for that region. This in fact means that what one country would call a heatwave, another might actually consider pleasantly cool conditions!

- The main danger to humans in a heatwave is hyperthermia (the overheating of the body) which is also known as heat stroke. Additionally, stress levels rise as heat increases, and this can affect the population more than you might expect – one interesting statistic is that there is a correlation between higher temperatures and greater levels of violent crime!

- In extreme heat conditions, wildfires – addressed elsewhere in this book – can be extremely problematic, with many posing a danger to human populations; additionally there can be increased risk of accidental damage when travelling as roads can buckle under the heat of the sun, weakening bridges. Furthermore, in countries where air conditioning is common, heatwaves can result in power outages as energy companies struggle to keep up with demand.

- Here is an interesting (although particularly morbid) fact. You may hear people talk (rather euphemistically) of something called the *harvesting effect* during a heatwave. This is the observation that in the weeks following a heatwave, mortality rates actually go down. The theory as to the reason for this is that older people and those that are more vulnerable who were *approaching* death had the end of their lives quickened by the heat, and thus aren't there to be measured as dying in the weeks when they were 'due'.

▶ Despite many other weather events being more visually impressive than a heatwave, it is in fact this type of weather that is America's biggest killer. In a ten-year period at the end of the last century, some 2190 people died as a direct result of excessive heat, whereas 'only' 880 died due to floods, and 150 because of hurricanes. Yet despite these awful figures, many people (in one study actually less than half) ignore the vast majority of advice given to them about actions to take in an impending heatwave, despite it being such simple things as 'drink plenty of water'.

▶ One of the most recent deadly heatwaves is that which occurred in India between April and May 2015. More than two thousand people died as daytime temperatures across millions of square miles of the country approached fifty degrees centigrade, almost ten degrees hotter than would normally have been expected.

▶ Australia's 2012-2013 summer is today called the *Angry Summer*; over a 90-day period over one hundred and twenty weather records were broken, including the country's hottest day ever – which is no mean feat, considering Australia is generally considered to be a pretty warm place! Wildfires caused destructions across huge areas of bush, and temperatures in some areas came close to fifty degrees centigrade.

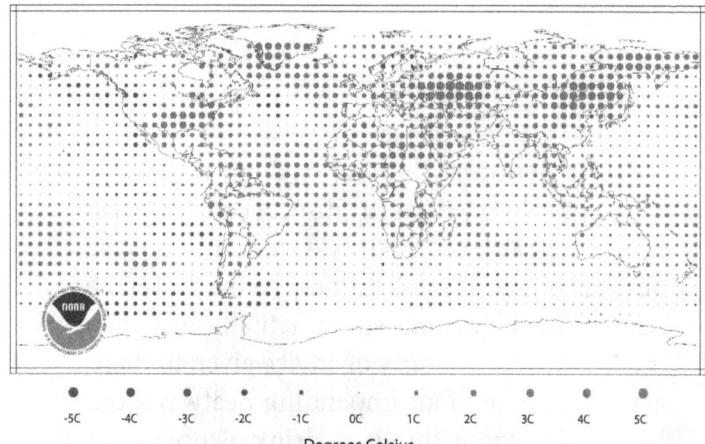

Temperature Anomalies June 2010
(with respect to a 1971-2000 base period)
National Climatic Data Center/NESDIS/NOAA

2010 saw much of the world experience unusually high temperatures.

- The early 1950s saw prolonged and severe drought in central and southern states of America, with some areas becoming drier than the *dustbowl* which had occurred twenty years before. East St. Louis, Illinois recorded a high of 47 degrees centigrade, the highest in the state to this very day.

- Also in the USA, the heatwaves of 1972 (in New York) and 1980 (across entire areas of central and Eastern states) both saw around one thousand people die in extreme temperatures coupled with very high levels of humidity. In the latter of these, Dallas saw an incredible forty-two consecutive days above 38 degrees centigrade, and the country as a whole saw its economy lose some $20 billion as a result of the debilitating heat. 1988 was worse in terms of lives lost however, with estimates of 17,000 deaths commonly suggested.

► Greece, another country famous for its heat (amongst many other things) experience an eleven-day heatwave in July 1987, with Athens hitting almost 42 degrees centigrade. This, coupled with extreme levels of humidity and very low wind speeds (even at night) saw comfort levels at an almost unbearable low.

Volcanoes

An eruption of the Mount Etna Volcano on the 31st of July 2011

- Volcanoes are ruptures in the surface of the earth (or other planets) that allow lava, volcanic ash and gas to escape. A volcanic eruption is caused when gas pressure builds up inside the volcano, eventually expelling out hot magma under enormous pressure.

- Many people think of volcanoes as fiery mountains, and although *some* fall into that category, there are many other types. Some volcanoes feature wide plateaus, other are bulging domes, and some are *fissure vents* – wide cracks from which lava emerges. Although it is normal to think of volcanoes as being on land, there are in fact many found on the ocean floor, and some even under the planet's icecaps!

- An *active* volcano is one that displays regular activity, from escape of gases or small lava flows to a full eruption. A *dormant* volcano is one that we know has had *some* historical activity, but is currently quiet. An *extinct* volcano is one that is never recorded in human history as having displayed activity and it is believed it will *never* erupt again.

- There are three different kinds of volcano. The first are known as *shield volcanoes*. These have lava flows with low viscosity (meaning they are thin and not very sticky) which flow for many miles. These volcanoes are therefore very wide and have smooth, shallow slopes. The second type, *stratovolcanoes*, are usually the largest. They can have many different types of eruption containing ash and rock, which means that they grow to astounding heights. The third type are *cinder cone volcanoes*. These are usually much smaller – only around 400m high – as their eruptions are very short-lived.

Krakatoa in 2008

- There are thought to be around 1500 active volcanoes in the world, based on the number that are known to have erupted in the last ten thousand years. However, some volcanologists point out that there *could* be thousands more on the sea bed of which we are unaware.

- *Huaynaputina*, a volcano in Peru, erupted in 1600 AD. The explosion was so powerful that it caused mud flows over seventy miles away. The ash cloud altered the world's climate to such an extent that the next few summers were the coldest in a five hundred year period.

- The *Ilopango Volcano* in El Salvador erupted so violently in 450 AD that most of the entire country was covered in volcanic material. Thousands of inhabitants of the early Mayan cities had to flee their homes, and their entire civilization changed from being one based in the highlands of El Salvador to the lowlands of Guatemala and the north of the country.

- The strongest explosion ever witnessed by humans is believed to be that of *Mount Thera* on the Island of Santorini in Greece. After studying the area, which was previously inhabited by the Minoan civilization, geologists say that in 1610 BC the volcano exploded with the energy of more than two hundred atomic bombs.

- On the border between China and North Korea lies *Changbaishan*, a volcano which erupted around one thousand years ago. So much pressure had built up that volcanic material was blown around seven hundred miles away to northern Japan.

- In 1815, *Mount Tambora* on Indonesia's Sumbawa Island erupted with devastating effects. Killing over seventy thousand people, the force seven explosion (known as 'super-colossal') was heard over a thousand miles away.

Lightning

- Lightning is the sudden flow of electricity that occurs during an electrical storm (which is also known as a *thunderstorm*). The flow can occur between different regions of the same cloud (known as *IC* or *intra-cloud lightning*), between two separate clouds (*CC lightning*) or between a cloud and the ground (*CG lightning*). When the flow discharges itself through an object on the ground, we refer to this as a *lightning strike*.

- Thunder is the sound of lightning, and you cannot have thunder *without* lightning. The sound itself is caused by the rapid expanding and contraction of air due to it being superheated by the electricity. By the way, don't think you're safe from lightning just because there are no clouds overhead. Lightning regularly strikes the ground over three miles from the centre of a thunderstorm (which can be much further than the furthest outreaches of cloud).

- A common myth about lightning is that it 'doesn't strike the same place twice'... this is completely and utterly untrue, and regularly hits the same place time after time, especially lightning conductors on tall buildings! A good example of this is the Empire State Building which is struck by lightning some one hundred times a year or more. Another myth is that the rubber tyres on a car protect you from a lightning strike; again this is not true. It is the metal 'cage' in which you sit that is the protection – this means that convertibles and fibreglass vehicles offer no protection from lightning!

- One of the most fascinating things about when lightning strikes a living person is that they are often scarred by branching tree-like patterns at the point they were hit. These fascinating patterns are called *Lichtenburg figures,* and you could say they were amongst the rarest – and most dangerous – body modifications one can undergo (although it is strongly suggested *not* to attempt to purposefully obtain these markings!) Those who survive being struck by lightning are very lucky to do so, especially when you consider that it is quite common for lightning to actually explode a tree when it strikes one – the reason for this is that the strike causes immense heat to travel through whatever object it strikes... in this case the tree's trunk, which contains sap. The sap is vaporised by the heat, and the pressure of this newly-expanded material is too much for the trunk to bear.

- Lightning strikes are dangerous to humans in many ways. Obviously striking an individual is normally a tragedy for that person. Lightning strikes can also cause fires that burn across thousands of acres of land, often threatening human settlements. Although aeroplanes are designed to cope structurally with a lightning strike, sometimes the electrical discharge causes the plane's electrical systems to fail, and with many modern aircraft designed solely as 'fly-by-wire', the result can be complete loss of control.

- A Park Ranger by the name of Roy Cleveland Sullivan from Virginia in the United States of America is listed by the Guinness Book of Records as the man struck by lightning on more recorded occasions than any other human being. On seven separate occasions Roy was struck by a bolt of lightning, and survived every single one. His nickname is given as either *The Human Lightning Rod* or *The Human Lightning Conductor* depending on which source you read. He was first struck in April 1942 whilst hiding from a thunderstorm in a fire lookout tower (the tower had no lightning rod). Roy said that *this* strike was the worst, burning a strip of flesh one and a half centimetres wide down his entire right leg and leaving a whole in his shoe! Twenty-seven years later he was hit again, this time whilst in his truck. Five more strikes followed over the next eight years. In one, Roy saw a cloud that seemed to be following him, so he ran away from it but kept up with him; after a while his pace slowed and a bolt of lightning shot out of the cloud and into his ankle. Astoundingly, this was actually the *second* cloud that Roy thought had directly targeted him with a lightning bolt!

▶ The deadliest lightning strike in modern times is that which struck LANSA (a Peruvian Airline) Flight 508 on the 24th of December 1971. When a bolt of lightning hit the plane, a Lockheed L-188A Electra turboprop, it crashed into the Amazon rainforest, killing six crew and eighty-five passengers. There were however eighty-six passengers on the flight. Incredibly, seventeen-year-old Juliane Koepcke fell two miles through the air whilst still strapped to her seat (which had been blasted out of the disintegrated plane) and survived the impact. She then walked through the jungle for ten days before she found some lumbermen who took her to hospital.

Lightning striking the city of Perth in Australia

▶ In 1769, a little over two hundred thousand pounds of gunpowder were stored in the vaults of the Church of the Nazaire in Brescia, Italy. The townspeople felt this was a pretty safe place to store it, however nature had other ideas. A particularly heavy thunderstorm in August saw a lightning bolt strike the tower. The current from the strike passed through the building and down to the vaults, where it ignited the huge stores of powder with devastating results – a sixth of the city was flattened, and some three thousand people were killed. As a direct result of this incident, the British parliament passed laws which controlled the manufacture and storage of gunpowder, ensuring that safety was taken into account.

- It doesn't take much to change a population from passive, law-abiding citizens to a baying mob... and lack of power tends to be a catalyst! New York City saw riots and looting in 1977 after a large number of lightning bolts struck the electrical transmission line in Westchester County, leaving inhabitants without power for more than twenty-four hours. Some described the scenes as 'apocalyptic', with people trapped in subways and elevators, and small fires breaking out all over the city.

- Lightning has even affected our attempts to conquer space. When a forty-metre long rocket and its cargo (together worth over 150 million dollars) was struck by lightning fifty-one seconds after launch, mission controllers had to order the unmanned vehicle to self-destruct. NASA were criticised for launching a rocket into storm clouds, although *they* blamed the Air Force for giving them an inaccurate weather report! This isn't the only time lightning jeopardised a space mission; back in 1969, Apollo 12 was struck by lightning half a minute after liftoff. All systems failed for a few moments, but to the great relief of the crew both on the rocket and on the ground, they came back online a few seconds later.

And Finally...

- Despite all of the terrible disasters you have read about in this book, the chances of something like this happening to you are extremely small. You can't live your life in fear of a natural disaster, but you should *respect* nature, understanding that the power of this planet is far in excess of that which we can wield as humans.

You may also enjoy...

You may also enjoy...

www.ingramcontent.com/pod-product-compliance
Lightning Source LLC
Chambersburg PA
CBHW031423040426
42444CB00005B/687